IT'S TIME TO EAT PINEAPPLES

It's Time to Eat PINEAPPLES

Walter the Educator

Silent King Books
A WhichHead Entertainment Imprint

Copyright © 2024 by Walter the Educator

All rights reserved. No part of this book may be reproduced in any manner whatsoever without written per- mission except in the case of brief quotations embodied in critical articles and reviews.

First Printing, 2024

Disclaimer

This book is a literary work; the story is not about specific persons, locations, situations, and/or circumstances unless mentioned in a historical context. Any resemblance to real persons, locations, situations, and/or circumstances is coincidental. This book is for entertainment and informational purposes only. The author and publisher offer this information without warranties expressed or implied. No matter the grounds, neither the author nor the publisher will be accountable for any losses, injuries, or other damages caused by the reader's use of this book. The use of this book acknowledges an understanding and acceptance of this disclaimer.

It's Time to Eat PINEAPPLES is a collectible early learning book by Walter the Educator suitable for all ages belonging to Walter the Educator's Time to Eat Book Series. Collect more books at WaltertheEducator.com

USE THE EXTRA SPACE TO TAKE NOTES AND DOCUMENT YOUR MEMORIES

PINEAPPLES

It's time to eat, let's gather near,

It's Time to Eat
Pineapples

A sunny fruit that brings us cheer!

It's golden yellow, juicy and sweet,

Hooray for pineapples, what a treat!

They grow on plants with spiky tops,

In sunny places, where raindrops stop.

Each one's a treasure, round and neat,

A tropical snack that's fun to eat.

Cut into rings, or chunks, or spears,

Pineapples bring us happy cheers.

They're tangy, tasty, and oh so fun,

A burst of flavor for everyone!

Take a bite, it's cool and bright,

It makes your mouth feel pure delight.

It's sweet and tart, the perfect mix,

Pineapple magic, a tasty fix!

It's Time to Eat
Pineapples

Add it to yogurt or eat it plain,

It's great in sunshine or even rain.

On pizza slices or in a stew,

Pineapples do so much for you!

The juice drips down, it's sticky, yes,

But every drop is happiness!

Just grab a napkin, clean your face,

Pineapple time's a yummy space.

They're healthy too, full of good things,

Like vitamins that make you sing.

They help you smile, they help you grow,

Pineapples are the way to go!

With friends or family, share a plate,

Pineapples make each moment great.

It's Time to Eat
Pineapples

Their golden color, their tropical flair,

Spread joy and sunshine everywhere.

So next time when it's snack-time call,

Choose pineapples, they're the best of all!

Juicy, golden, fresh, and bright,

Pineapples make everything right.

Let's clap and cheer, hooray, hooray!

For pineapples bring a sunny day.

Each bite's a treat, so full of fun,

It's Time to Eat
Pineapples

Pineapple time for everyone!

ABOUT THE CREATOR

Walter the Educator is one of the pseudonyms for Walter Anderson. Formally educated in Chemistry, Business, and Education, he is an educator, an author, a diverse entrepreneur, and he is the son of a disabled war veteran. "Walter the Educator" shares his time between educating and creating. He holds interests and owns several creative projects that entertain, enlighten, enhance, and educate, hoping to inspire and motivate you. Follow, find new works, and stay up to date with Walter the Educator™

at WaltertheEducator.com

www.ingramcontent.com/pod-product-compliance
Lightning Source LLC
LaVergne TN
LVHW052014060526
838201LV00059B/4024